6/20
$30.71

Major League SOCCER

Colorado Rapids

Marty Gitlin

Printing   1   2   3   4   5   6   7   8

First Edition, 2020.
Author: Marty Gitlin
Designer: Ed Morgan
Editor: Lisa Petrillo

Series: Major League Soccer
Title: Colorado Rapids / by Marty Gitlin

Hallandale, FL : Mitchell Lane Publishers, [2020]

Library bound ISBN: 9781680204865
eBook ISBN: 9781680204872

Contents

Words in **bold** throughout
can be found in the Glossary.

A Study of Major League Soccer

CHAPTER ONE

There was little room for most Americans on the sports calendar. They loved football. And baseball. And basketball. They were not interested in soccer.

They knew it was the most popular sport in the world. They knew it was played by more than 265 million people in 200 nations. But they were too busy watching other sports to give it much attention.

Then came the 1990s. The number of soccer fans and players in the United States grew. Kids began booting soccer balls in youth leagues around the country. Folks who never dreamed of watching soccer began tuning into **international** matches on television.

The Rose Bowl in Pasadena, California is packed on Sunday, July 17, 1994 as fireworks offer a prelude to the final match of the XV World Cup.

It all began when U.S. soccer officials made a trade in 1988 with FIFA, which runs the sport worldwide. FIFA stands for the Fédération Internationale de Football Association, which is French for International Federation of Association Football. And it offered the United States an opportunity to host the World Cup for the first time in 1994. But the powerful organization overseeing the world of professional soccer had one demand. The U.S. had to launch its own professional soccer league.

Major League Soccer was born. It took eight more years to organize. It began play in 1996 with 10 teams. Not every major U.S. city boasted a **franchise**. Even the huge city of Chicago was without one.

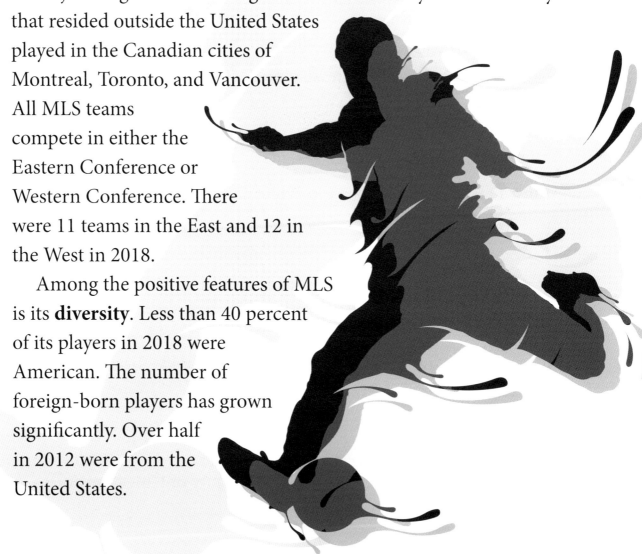

Fans came out in droves. An average of 17,406 attended MLS games that year. And the number continued to rise. It jumped by 5,000 over the next five years and rose to 22,113 in 2017.

No team gained more popularity than the Seattle Sounders. They averaged more than 40,000 fans per home game during that period. Folks also streamed into the stadium to watch the Atlanta Football Club. A league-best 48,200 fans attended its matches in its first season of 2017.

Major League Soccer had grown to 23 teams by 2018. The only three that resided outside the United States played in the Canadian cities of Montreal, Toronto, and Vancouver. All MLS teams compete in either the Eastern Conference or Western Conference. There were 11 teams in the East and 12 in the West in 2018.

Among the positive features of MLS is its **diversity**. Less than 40 percent of its players in 2018 were American. The number of foreign-born players has grown significantly. Over half in 2012 were from the United States.

California easily boasts the most U.S.-born MLS players with 71. New York is a distant second with 21 and Texas third with 18.

Each MLS team plays 34 matches. They are divided equally between battles at home and on the road. They receive three points for every victory and one for a tie. Those that finish among the top six in their conference land a **playoff** spot. The two that compile the most points claim a bye in the first round. That allows them to advance to the second round while the other teams must win a match to stay alive.

The next two rounds feature two-match playoffs. The teams that score the most goals in those matches compete for the **MLS Cup** title in December. That ends a long season that starts in March. But all those tough battles are worth it, especially for the team that snags the crown. One team that knows all about winning a crown is the Colorado Rapids.

Fun Facts

1 No Canadian team won an MLS title until the Toronto Football Club snagged it in 2017. Toronto beat the defending champion Seattle Sounders to take the crown.

2 The MLS will boast 26 teams by 2020. That is the year it will add franchises in Cincinnati, Nashville, and Miami. The league will have added 16 teams since it was launched in 1996.

A Rapid History

It was November 21, 2010. The Colorado Rapids and FC Dallas were competing for the MLS championship. Regulation time had ended in a 1–1 tie. So had the first period of extra time. The tension at BMO Field in Toronto was mounting. The pressure on the players was incredible.

Colorado Rapids forward Macoumba Kandji moved the ball from his right foot to his left. He booted it between the legs of FC Dallas defender Jair Benitez. He pushed Benitez aside and kicked the ball forward.

He had no chance to score. He was standing to the side of the goal. Kandji just hoped to find a teammate that could slam the ball in. He got lucky. The ball bounced off Dallas defender George John and past goalkeeper Kevin Hartman. The Rapids won 2–1. Kandji helped his team capture its first MLS crown.

Macoumba Kandji (*10*) is crowed by his team after scoring the game winning goal as FC Dallas defender Ugo Ihemelu (bottom) looks on in November 2010.

Kandji tore a knee ligament on the play. But he would trade an injury for a championship any day. After all, the Rapids were a charter member of MLS. And they had never won a title. They had not even reached the playoffs the previous three seasons.

The Rapids players did make the finals in 1997. They embarked on an amazing run after barely qualifying for the playoffs with a 14–18 record. They scored just 50 goals in 32 games during the regular season. But they tallied six in two games to beat Kansas City in the first round. The Rapids then upset FC Dallas to earn a chance at the championship before falling to D.C. United.

Colorado has never placed first in the Western Conference. Its highest finish was second in 2016. But the Rapids have often risen to the occasion in the playoffs. They reached the **semifinals** in 2002 despite barely winning more games than they lost. They did not finish over .500 in 2005 or 2006 but made the semifinals in both years. They qualified for the playoffs in 13 of their 20 seasons through 2017.

The Rapids have not been content to look the same year after year. The franchise used green as its primary uniform color, then switched to black and blue starting in 2003. They changed to burgundy and blue in 2007.

The team has also boasted a variety of logos. The original featured the Colorado River as its primary crest. The team has used a logo since 2007 featuring the Rocky Mountains and the number 96 to honor its **inaugural** season of 1996.

Midfielder Kellyn Acosta plays in the second half of an MLS soccer match against FC Dallas in October 2018. The Rapids won 2-1.

Colorado shared Mile High Stadium (renamed Invesco Field) with the NFL Denver Broncos from 1996 to 2006. The Rapids team members wanted a smaller **venue** of their own. The result was a move to brand new Dick's Sporting Goods Park in suburban Commerce Park in 2007. Their home stadium can hold as many as 18,061 fans.

The Rapids attracted many crowds numbering larger than 50,000 when they played at Mile High. A throng of 61,202 fans streamed in to watch Colorado defeat Chicago on July 4, 2002. It remains the largest single-game attendance in franchise history. The Rapids have not consistently sold out Dick's Sporting Goods Park. But they have averaged more than 15,000 fans per home game since 2012.

Those fans have enjoyed Major League Soccer. Many of them have learned more about the sport by attending those matches.

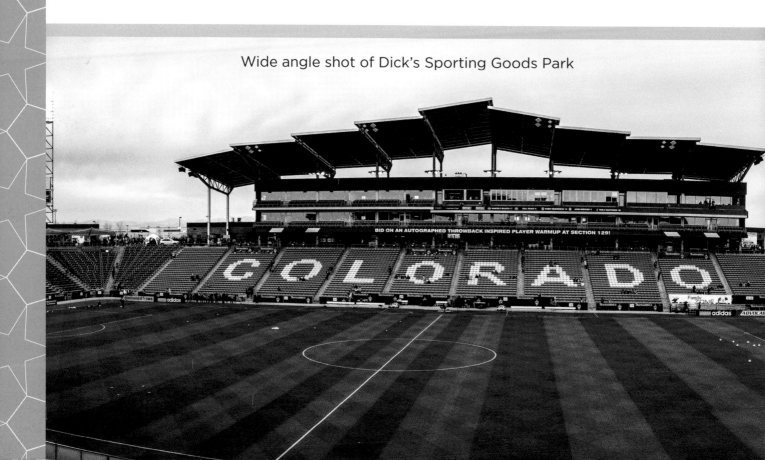
Wide angle shot of Dick's Sporting Goods Park

Fun Facts

1 The Rapids made an incredible turnaround at home in 2016. They had posted only their second losing record in home matches in 2015 with a 5-7-5 mark. But they compiled an 11-0-6 mark at Dick's Sporting Goods Park in 2016.

2 Colorado improved as a team in each of its first four seasons. Team members posted an 11-21-2 mark in their first season of 1996. They were 14–18 in 1997, 16–16 in 1998, and 20–12 in 1999.

The Players and Positions

CHAPTER THREE

Imagine you are a defender in Major League Soccer. You are the last line of defense between your opponent and your goalkeeper. Your team is winning 1–0. There is just one minute remaining in the match. And the top scorer on the other team is coming right at you.

He is passing the ball from one foot to the other. You are the only player on the field standing between him and the net. He kicks the ball to the right. You bolt in that direction. He takes his leg back and slams the ball. It is headed to the right corner of the net. There is no way the goalkeeper can stop it.

You thrust your leg to the left just in time. The ball bounces off your foot and rolls harmlessly away. A fellow defender boots it downfield. You have saved the victory.

Goalkeeper(GK)
Right back defender (RB)
Left back defender (LB)
Center back defender (CB)
Left midfielder (LM)
Center midfielder (CM)
Right midfielder (RM)
Left forward (LF)
Right forward (RF)

Soon you are celebrating with your teammates. All of them contributed to the win. Included among the defenders were the three midfielders. They roamed around the middle of the field while the two wingbacks played along the sidelines.

You are one of two center-backs who defend around midfield closer to the net. You are helped by two fullbacks who defend near the sidelines. They have all made it an easy night for the goalkeeper. He was required to stop just three easy shots on goal.

Everyone else on the field helped on offense. Included were the center midfielders, who played both offense and defense. The attacking midfielder worked to control the ball and **assisted** on the goal.

Those goals are most often scored by wings and forwards. They play closest to the net and try to boot the ball in when given the chance. One of the forwards scored the only goal of the match by slamming the ball off his head. Those shots are called headers. You know that the forwards receive the most attention because they score the most goals. But you also know that you saved the game with your play.

The battle that night was against one of your team's biggest rivals. **Rivalries** in Major League Soccer are based on one of two factors. The first is geography. Franchises located in nearby cities often forge heated rivalries. Another is playoff history. Teams that battle each other for the title also spark rivalries.

The Rapids consider Sporting Kansas City their biggest rival. Most matches between the two teams have been close. Colorado owns a 17–21 mark against Kansas City with 13 ties.

Midfielder Jack McBean (*right*) controls the ball in front of Sporting Kansas City defender Ike Opara in May 2018.

Like most teams, the Rapids have struggled on the road. They own an 81-204-63 mark away from home since 1996. They have finished under .500 on the road every season since 1999, when they managed a 9–7 mark. They have since won more than four road matches only once. They bottomed out in 2017 with a 1–14–2 record away from home.

The Rapids have definitely played better in front of their own supporters. The cheering fans give them energy. So do their fun mascots. The team has unveiled several mascots since moving to its new park in 2007. Included were Edson the Eagle, Franz the Fox, a bison named Marco von Bison, and a raccoon named Jorge el Mapache.

But the players are the Rapids' real stars. And they have boasted some of the best in MLS history.

Fun Facts

1 Some U.S. sports fans complain that soccer teams rarely score more than three goals. That is true. There has been only one exception in an MLS Cup final. San Jose tallied four goals to beat Chicago in 2003.

2 The Rapids would boast a winning record against Sporting Kansas City if not for their overtime matches. They have lost all six against their rivals.

Bravo for Bravo and Many More

When Rapids fans yelled "Bravo" during games, they were not just cheering. They were screaming out the name of their favorite player. And that was midfielder Paul Bravo, who played for the team from 1997 to 2001.

The California native remains one of the top scorers ever for the Rapids. His 39 goals rank second in team history and his 21 assists place him eighth. He performed his best under pressure. Bravo exploded for three goals and two assists during the team's run to the finals in 1997 and added two scores in the 2000 playoffs.

Bravo stayed atop the all-time Rapids scoring list until fellow American Conor Casey came along. The talented forward wore a Colorado uniform from 2007 to 2012. His finest seasons were from 2006 to 2008, when he racked up 40 goals.

Conor Casey (*center*) goes for a head ball between New England Revolution's Darrius Barnes (*left*) and Jeff Larentowicz in May 2009.

Casey finished his Rapids career with 50 goals. Nobody else in franchise history is even close. Casey peaked when he won the MLS Player of the Month award in May 2009 and earned a spot on the all-star team that year. He also tallied two goals during the 2010 playoff blitz that resulted in a championship.

Canadian midfielder Mark Chung arrived in Colorado after six years in Major League Soccer. He turned 32 years old during his first season with the Rapids. But that left him plenty of time to become one of the top players to ever wear their uniform. Chung enjoyed the best seasons of his career in Colorado. He scored 11 goals in 2002 and 2003. He became the first finalist for MLS Most Valuable Player honors in franchise history in 2002.

It is rare for a Major League Soccer star to emerge from the state of Idaho. But the premier goalkeeper ever to play for the Rapids did come from that state: Joe Cannon. Cannon allowed an average of just 1.26 goals per game during his time with the team from 2003 to 2006. He pitched 25 **shutouts** and set the franchise record with 349 saves. Cannon was honored for his greatness. He won MLS Goalkeeper of the Year in 2004 and was a finalist for the award in 2005 and 2006.

Goalkeeper Joe Cannon blocks a shot on goal against FC Dallas in the 2006 MLS Western Conference semifinal playoff series.

Not all Rapids standouts came from the United States or Canada. Among their best foreign-born players was forward Omar Cummings of Jamaica. Cummings graced the field for Colorado from 2007 to 2013. He is tied for second in team history with 39 goals and fourth in assists with 26. He recorded two playoff assists to help the Rapids capture the MLS crown in 2010.

Omar Cummings (*front*) fights off Carlyle Mitchell of the Vancouver Whitecaps in October 2011.

Another who came a long way was defender Pablo Mastroeni. He was born in Argentina but moved to the United States at the age of four. He joined the Rapids after four years with Miami and stuck around from 2002 to 2013. He set the all-time team mark with 225 games and nearly 19,000 minutes played.

Player Axel Sjoberg came from Sweden to tally only one goal for the Rapids in 2016. But the defender performed so well in preventing scores that he was voted onto the MLS Best 11 team that year.

Many of the top Colorado players spent most of their lives in other countries. The journey of foreign-born players in MLS is an exciting one. But making the change is quite a challenge.

Fun Facts

1 Joe Cannon is considered the greatest goalkeeper in Rapids history. But he only ranks second in goals against average. Bouna Coundoul from the African nation of Senegal allowed just 1.16 goals per game for Colorado from 2006 to 2008.

2 No Rapids player tallied more assists than Chris Henderson. The midfielder played for Colorado from 1996 to 1998, then returned from 2002 to 2005. His 53 assists is easily a team record.

The Tough Transition

CHAPTER FIVE

Many soccer players join MLS teams every year in the United States and Canada. They must move to another country. But it feels like they are moving to another world.

They arrive from all over the globe to play Major League Soccer. They come from South America. Or Africa. Or Europe. They embrace competing in an international sport.

But the transition is not easy. Some of those new to the United States do not speak English. They have never set foot on American soil. They have never seen cities as large as New York, Los Angeles, or Chicago. It can be overwhelming.

The number of foreign-born players in MLS keeps growing. Only about four of every 10 minutes on the field in 2017 was spent by a U.S.-born player. That was down significantly from 2013.

Most foreign players travel thousands of miles from their homes. Their new country is a strange place to them. Adapting to daily life is tougher than kicking a ball or stopping it from going into a net.

The challenges are many. They must learn a new language. They yearn to see their families back home. Everyone they meet is a stranger. They must seek out a new place to live. They cannot understand their teammates or coaches. They must buy items with bills and coins they had never seen.

Those who bring their families to the United States at least have familiar company. But their wives and kids face the same uphill battles. Their adjustment is especially hard if they do not speak English.

The soccer field should provide comfort for foreign players. It often does not. Even their teammates are strangers at first. It takes time to learn the strengths and weaknesses of new opponents. They often have nobody to talk to in their own language. That makes it impossible to recognize coaching commands or communicate with teammates. They cannot even reply to questions from the media without an **interpreter**.

Traveling in an unfamiliar land can feel strange. The United States and Canada are two of the largest countries in the world. Most foreign players are from much smaller nations. They are used to traveling short distances to matches on buses or trains. They must **adapt** to long plane trips and sleeping in hotels.

Time spent away from home can be far tougher on foreign players. MLS teams often play on Saturday nights. But they must leave for their destinations on Thursday or Friday. Matches end late. Players do not return home until Sunday. Such travels are usually easy for American and Canadian players. The experience might be terrible for those unused to the **culture**.

Every city can be an adventure. Foreign players must even adjust to the weather. The weather is often the same throughout smaller countries. Such is not the case in the United States and Canada. MLS teams might play a Wednesday match in rainy Seattle. Three days later they could be in snowy Toronto. And the following week they might be playing in the sizzling heat of Texas.

Foreign players are forced to adapt on the field to more than Mother Nature. Pace of play is faster in MLS than in most international competitions. Matches are won with talent. The best athletes succeed in MLS. **Strategy** is limited. Those from other nations often struggle until they get used to the speed of the game.

Adjusting to a new world and new game takes time. But foreign players have much in common with their teammates. They both boast great talent and a love for soccer. Those from other countries have helped the Colorado Rapids win playoff matches and an MLS crown. And they have made Major League Soccer truly an international game.

Fun Facts

1 Major League Soccer received plenty of publicity in 2007. That is when international superstar David Beckham entered the league by joining the Los Angeles Galaxy. He led that team to two championships before retiring in 2013.

2 Pablo Mastroeni was not away long after leaving the Rapids as a player in 2013. He returned to coach the team in 2014. Mastroeni remained in that position until 2017. Colorado struggled during his tenure but did post a 15-6-13 record in 2015.

ou **Should Know**

ccer-like game was used to train Chinese soldiers 2,000 yea

ent Greeks and Romans also played a sport like soccer.

game as it is now played probably started in England more t s ago. It celebrated a victory in battle over invaders from Ro

4, British King Edward II made playing soccer illegal.

Rapids lost their first-ever match in Kansas City on April 13, won their first home match eight days later. They beat the D 3-1, in front of 21,711 fans.

rado placed last in the Western Conference in the first MLS s Rapids lost nine of their last 11 matches that year.

argest home crowd of nearly every MLS season from 1996 to a Rapids victory. They were 12-1 in those games. The lone ex a loss to Columbus in 1999. Oddly, that was the year they ma best record during that stretch.

only MLS Rookie of the Year in Rapids history was Dillon Pov elder scored five goals and added six assists in 2013 to earr d. He remained with the team through 2017.

Quick Stats

The 2009 Rapids finished with an odd regular season record of 10-10-10

Colorado owned an all-time playoff record of 14-22-4 through 2017

The Rapids have allowed a franchise-low 32 goals in four seasons, including in the championship year of 2010

1995 Colorado receives one of the first 10 franchises for the inaugural year of Major League Soccer.

1997 The Rapids earn a spot in the MLS Cup finals despite finishing 14-18 in the regular season. They fall to D.C. United in the championship round.

1999 Colorado finishes the regular season with a 20-12 record. That would remain their largest win total through 2017.

2004 Joe Cannon wins MLS Goalkeeper of the Year honors and is a finalist for the League's Most Valuable Player award.

2007 The Rapids move from Invesco Field to smaller Dick's Sporting Goods Park. They are no longer sharing a stadium with the NFL Denver Broncos.

2010 Coach Gary Smith and his Rapids win their first MLS Cup championship. They clinch the crown with a 2-1 victory over Dallas as Macoumba Kandji scores the game-winner in extra time.

2014 Pablo Mastroeni takes over as Rapids coach after a long stint with the team as a player. But Colorado finishes his first season with just eight wins. It is the team's lowest victory total since 2001.

2016 The Rapids compile the best winning percentage in franchise history. They finish the regular season with a 15-6-13 mark but lose to Toronto in the knockout round of the playoffs.

Glossary

adapt
A change to make life better or easier

assist
A pass that leads directly to a goal scored

culture
The ways of living in a particular country

diversity
Different kinds of people

franchise
A sports organization that features a team

inaugural
The first ever

international
Anything to do with more than one country

interpreter
Person who translates the words of another speaking a different language

MLS Cup
The championship match in Major League Soccer

playoffs
Series of sports games or matches held after the regular season to determine a champion

rivalries
Higher level of competitive fire between teams

semifinals
A series of games or matches to determine the two finalists that compete for a title

shutout
Holding an opponent without a goal

strategy
A careful plan or method

venue
Place where an event is held

Further Reading

Gitlin, Marty. *Neymar: Soccer Superstar*. Chicago, Illinois: Britannica Educational Publishing, 2018.

Latham, Andrew. *Soccer Smarts for Kids: 60 Skills, Strategies, and Secrets*. Rockridge Press, 2016.

Roth, B.A. *David Beckham: Born to Play*. New York, New York: Grosset and Dunlap, 2007.

On the Internet

MLS Next
https://www.mlssoccer.com/next
This website details the future of Major League Soccer.

Colorado Rapids
http://www.coloradorapids.com/
This official Rapids site features photos, team news, videos, and statistics.

Pablo Mastroeni profile
https://www.mlssoccer.com/players/pablo-mastroeni
Learn about the Rapids longtime player and coach on this site.

Index

About the Author

Marty Gitlin has authored more than 140 educational books. He has written dozens of sports books, including several about soccer stars. He has taken a special interest in Major League Soccer and the history of the Colorado Rapids. Gitlin spent 11 years as a newspaper sportswriter and won more than 45 awards during that time. Among them was a first place for general excellence from the Associated Press. That organization also selected him as one of the top four feature writers in Ohio.